25
Top Sales
Techniques

Dedication

To JZ and IZ

25
Top Sales
Techniques

Stephan Schiffman

**KOGAN
PAGE**

Acknowledgments

I would like to thank the following people for their help with this book: Brandon Toropov; Michele Reisner, for her aid in developing the original concept; Lynne Einleger for her encouragement; and, of course, Anne, Daniele, and Jennifer for their unceasing support.

Copyright © Stephan Schiffman 1991

First published in the United States of America in 1991 by Bob Adams Inc, 260 Center Street, Holbrook, Massachusetts 02343, USA.

This edition first published in Great Britain in 1992
by Kogan Page Ltd, 120 Pentonville Road, London N1 9JN.
Reprinted 1994

British Library Cataloguing in Publication Data

A CIP record for this book is available from the British Library.

ISBN 0-7494-0736-0

£8.76

Typeset by DP Photosetting, Aylesbury, Bucks
Printed and bound in Great Britain by
Clays Ltd, St Ives plc.

Contents

Technique 1:
Communicating the Message that It is Sound Business to Trust You

I've trained over a quarter of a million sales people. And the more sales people I run into, the more exposure I get to various 'tricks of the trade' – little corners that sales people sometimes cut in order to get ahead (or so they think) in the short term. The only problem is, too many of these tricks of the trade undercut an essential objective: that of constantly sending and reinforcing the message that it is a good business decision to trust you.

I know a car dealer who uses such a trick to get people to come into his showroom. He opens up the telephone directory, finds a name, calls the person, and says, 'Hi, Mr Jones, this is Mike Johnson at Johnson Used Cars. You've just won our raffle! Come in and collect a turkey!' What he never says is that he really wants the person to come and collect two turkeys: one to put in the oven, and the other to drive away in. (By the way, there is no raffle; the turkeys are bought as premiums for anyone who walks in the door.)

The same salesperson would call up someone at random and claim to have found his wallet, 'just to get his attention', then launch into his pitch. How much would you trust an approach like that?

I'm not trying to be harsh towards those people who sell cars for a living. Some of the most effective sales people I know sell used cars. But I am trying to say something about this used car salesman: by starting off with 'Hi, you've won a free turkey,' he was using a cheap trick. It seems to me that it was no coincidence that he sold cars to match. Word gets around about that sort of thing.

If you sell turkeys, talk about turkeys. If you sell cars, talk about cars; talk about exactly why it makes perfect sense to trust you enough to buy the one you have to offer.

Beware of the tricks of the trade. If they come at the expense of your credibility, they're too expensive.

To be trusted, you must be trustworthy. Too many sales people focus on whether or not they have learned to appear trustworthy. That's not the point! You want to develop an earned reputation for following through on everything – and I mean every syllable – that comes out of your mouth. That can start with phoning at 9.00 am, and not 8.58 or 9.02 am, if you say that's when you'll phone. Some sales people take this principle and turn it into a recipe for annoyance; others display the spark of professionalism necessary to demonstrate dependability and consistency as personal hallmarks.

If you think such 'minor details' don't have any real persuasive power, I have to disagree with you. At the beginning of your relationship with a prospect, they are all he has to go on. They are the only tool you have. Promise the moon, and you'll be like every other salesperson. Say you're now ready to fax over a quote – within the next five minutes, guaranteed – that completely meets all the prospect's specifications, then do it, and you're one in a million.

Relationships are built on trust, and trust is built on evidence of all kinds. This does not mean that you must show you are subservient – that will have the opposite of the effect you desire. Demonstrate that you are unfailingly dependable in all things, big and small, and make a habit of delivering what you have promised (or, preferably, more). You will win both trust and sales as a result.

Technique 2:
Asking the Right Questions

Ask important questions. Ask real questions. If you need to rely on 'How's the weather?' or 'Have a nice weekend?' for your opening, fine. But thereafter, base everything you ask on a simple principle: *never waste the prospect's time*. That may seem like an obvious point, but it certainly isn't treated like one by most sales people! Know when it's time to move beyond the litany of pointless observations on decor, golf, the weather or whatever. You came here on a business appointment. There will come a point at which your client will be ready to move past the small talk. Do so, tactfully.

How do you start asking the important questions? I'm going to suggest that you start with a simple one – a question that may seem to have nothing to do with your visit, but that will actually yield some remarkable insights into the kind of person you're working with.

'Just out of curiosity, Ms Allen – how did you get this job?'

That will ease you into the 'business end' of the visit quite nicely, and will also encourage your contact to open up to you. After your prospect has had the chance to answer in whatever degree of detail he or she feels comfortable with, you might continue by saying what you have in mind – why you're talking to the person the first place – and explaining why you're going over this (so your later questions will make more sense).

'Ms Allen, we handle the top-selling line of widgets in the United Kingdom. Let me tell you a little bit about how we work. My only job during this first meeting is to find out about your needs; I didn't come here to sell anything today. I mention that because I wanted to ask you a few questions about your business to find out if I really can help you to boost your sales volume. Have you got a moment for that?'

Assuming you get a 'yes' (and that's a pretty good bet), you can then move on to the big questions.

(Question 1. The Past:) 'Have you ever used any of our widgets before?' ('If so, how did they work out?')

(Question 2. The Present:) 'Just out of curiosity, what widget are you using now?' ('How do you feel about it?')

(Question 3. The Future:) 'Tell me something; what do the next six months look like for you in terms of widget use?' ('How do you plan to use widgets to reach goal x?')

If you feel uncomfortable moving into 'serious' areas, like whether or not the firm uses or might use your products, but you still feel certain that you have passed the point at which you can discuss last night's football match, there are a number of middle-ground questions you can pose before getting to the heart of the matter. Here are some suggestions.

'Tell me, what kind of customers do you serve?'

'What other branches do you have?' (Or: 'Where are your headquarters located?')

'What kind of sales force do you use?'

'How long has the firm been in business?'

'What kind of challenges do you face in this business/industry?'

Such questions may yield important information for you, and can serve as an effective bridge to the main point of your visit. But beware of over-reliance on such middle-ground questions; my guess is that your contact is, like most of us these days, short of time. Most prospects will appreciate your getting to the point without delay, and you can do this without jeopardising the emerging relationship.

The last 'right question' of your first visit usually sounds something like this:

'You know, Mr Jones, I've learned a lot today, and I'd like to thank you for talking to me. Let me tell you what I usually do at this stage. I think we're at that point now where I need to set up another appointment for us, one where I can come back after having sorted out everything I've learned here and show you what we may be able to do for your company. Is Tuesday at three all right?'

Technique 3:
Taking the Lead

Tell the prospect where you are at any given point in the sales cycle. Don't be afraid to steer the conversation in the direction you want it to go.

> *'Mr Prospect, I want to thank you for taking time to see me today. I know we have a lot to go over, but during this part of the visit what I usually do is give some information about my company and what we do. We've been in business since . . .'*

> *'Mr Prospect, at this stage I'd like to ask a couple of simple questions that will help me to find out ways we can help you.'*

> *'Well, now that we've come this far, Mr Prospect, I'll tell you what I'd like to do. I'd like to take these notes and go back to my office and see if we can work out a proposal for you, then meet again next week. Would Friday at two be all right?'*

> *'Certainly good to meet you again, Mr Prospect. Now that we've worked out this proposal, I think it would be a good idea for me to take a few minutes to just summarise it for you here, and then answer any questions you may have.'*

> *'So that's our proposal, Mr Prospect. I have a feeling we will really be able to put this programme into place for you successfully. At this point in the process, my feeling is that the sooner we get this under way, the better it will be for your*

company. Is Saturday the twelfth of December a good day to start?'

How many presentations are sabotaged by sales people who want to avoid 'offending' – and never get around to mentioning the reason they stepped in the door in the first place? Take charge. Make a conscious choice to inform the prospect with regard to where you both are in the process. The alternative is long, 'good' meetings that end in that odd, result-free limbo that leaves neither party sure what to do next.

We don't live in a perfect world. We live in a world of complex people who have complex thinking patterns – people whose next action may not be obvious to us. It follows, then, that we run the risk of having the prospect stop us and say, 'Hold on – wait a minute. I'm not ready for that yet. You're moving too fast for me.'

So what do you do now?

You need that information. You need to know where there is still a problem to be worked on. If you don't know where there's a problem, you won't be able to close the sale. And it's far better to isolate a problem through a consistent system of 'sequence updates' (as I like to call them) than to wait until the last minute, ask for the business, and then find out there was something important you should have been paying attention to but weren't.

Sometimes, as a result of these updates and the feedback you receive from them, you will isolate needs the prospect has not yet brought to the surface. You may find that, even though you went in the door thinking about selling Widget A, and even though the prospect seems interested enough in Widget A, the questions that keep coming up as you try to move the process along seem to concern the applications you know can only be obtained through Widget B! Your objective is to solve problems, to satisfy needs – not to make the prospect fit your preconceptions! So you move on to Widget B. But you can only do this because you've listened to the feedback your updates have yielded.

Let's be clear on one thing: sales cycles will vary from industry to industry and from customer to customer. What that means in plain English is that you never know when someone's going to agree to buy something. I'm not suggesting that you try to manhandle the prospect. Even if you issue the updates I'm talking about, you still have to be willing to work with the prospect, every step of the way. The key point is, you can't do that unless you both know where you are – and where you're going.

Technique 4:
Engaging the Prospect

Engaging the prospect is a subtle undertaking; it is difficult to define. I should start out by telling you what it's not. Engaging the prospect is not reacting instantaneously, as if by reflex, to every comment or perceived disapproval. Consider this exchange.

Prospect: The last time we worked in this area, I'll never forget, the first session was on a Monday morning, and . . .
You: Oh, we can work on Mondays. Mondays are no problem.
Prospect: Well, actually, what I was going to say was that since it was a Monday morning, we didn't have quite the eager spirit that we might have . . .
You: I see, I see. Well, we can do it on any day you want.

That's not engaging anyone. That's ping-pong. Engaging your prospect means going beyond slapshot, automatic exchanges. It requires that you so clearly respond to stated or unstated needs (not all of which will have to do with your product or service) that you establish a core of understanding and a framework within which both you and your prospect can solve important problems.

21

You will have to find, for yourself, the best way to establish that connection, given the particular dynamics of a given prospect's age, position, gender or even race, in comparison with yours. It is pointless to ignore such differences among people, and virtually suicidal not to accommodate them in a sales setting.

Every prospect is different. Every prospect reacts differently to what you have to say. Some seem to have all the time in the world, others consider a 15-minute meeting to be a major crisis in time management. Some have made careers out of being sceptical, others pride themselves on freethinking, even outrageous approaches to problems. The point is, you cannot earn the respect of all of them with a single 'script' designed to 'handle the first few minutes'. You must identify what is important to any given prospect, then learn how to appeal to those values.

Here are some general suggestions on drawing out your prospect and initiating meaningful initial conversations. Of course, you will have to adapt them to fit particular situations.

Discuss objects you are comfortable and familiar with. Avoid venturing opinions on Abstract Expressionism if you know nothing about that branch of modern art; do offer your insights on model trains, Disney collectibles or memory improvement if the topic in question is one you have an informed interest in. Your confidence in the subject you select – and connect somehow to your prospect – will carry over. (*Note:* There is an advantage to beginning an exchange by focusing on your own observations and experiences – adroitly and tactfully, of course. Doing so takes some of the pressure off your prospect, who will be expecting you to try to 'draw him in'.)

Discuss the surroundings. The office you will be sitting in is a reflection of its occupant. Surely you can find, with little difficulty, something that will serve as a positive conversational starting point that has to do with the way your prospect has chosen to decorate his or her surroundings.

When the person starts to talk about himself, 'lean in' to the conversation. I also put down the pen I'm using to take notes. This serves as a subtle validator that the prospect's experiences are inherently interesting. (It is virtually always good to get the prospect discussing his or her own experiences. People who talk about themselves are more relaxed than people who don't.)

Show care by really caring. Remember, you're there to help. When the prospect outlines a problem, show the same concern you would if it were yours. (After all, you want it to be yours!)

Technique 5:
Finding Key Requirements

Should you set your goal as that of 'finding customers who need the product'? All the time? The answer is more complicated than you might think.

Most of us who are selling today are not creating a new market. That is to say, we're not following the time-honoured advice to 'find a need and fill it', because, on the whole, we can't. Our economy has been eradicating basic needs on an historically unprecedented scale for almost half a century now, and it's done a pretty good job. Not a perfect job, of course, but a good enough job to change the way most sales people must operate. What today's sales people must do is find *requirements* they can fill among those sought-after, qualified buyers who know full well that the choice is theirs when it comes to choosing the new widget service.

We have a lot of cars in this country. We have a lot of copiers. And we have a variety of pension plans available, too. If it is your job to sell a car, a copier or a pension plan, you will have to come up with something new and exciting about your particular offer for a given buyer who, these days, can more and more be counted on to have some experience of your product or service category. You will have to tailor your approach to the requirements you identify within such prospect groups. Otherwise, you will have some problems.

This is not to say there is no such thing as a first-time car buyer, or a company that is shopping around for its first pension plan. Obviously, the patterns of 'new' buyers will vary from region to region and from industry to industry. My point is, most good sales people I meet do not make 'virgin' prospects their core concern. Their objective, typically, is not to identify a need for the widget, but to get an idea of the type of widget buyer/user whose needs they can satisfy better than anyone else – then make some striking comparisons to that person.

Find your segment, your area of expertise, your niche. Learn to classify common concerns and problems shared by the types of 'educated' customers you know you have been able to satisfy. Then prospect for that person. Of course, you aren't going to turn anyone down who doesn't fit your profile and still wants to buy from you. But most successful sales people I know develop a sense of who the likely customer is – and then put themselves in front of as many of those types of people as possible.

With someone who's been using Brand X widgets for 20 years, your goal will not be identifying the need – it will be unearthing the requirements that will have to be met before your prospect will consider changing to your Brand Y widgets.

Does he require a better service plan? More flexibility with payments? A better price? Frequent contact with you, the salesperson. There are a million variations. Often the requirements will be difficult to gauge;

perhaps the prospect himself has not fully identified them. That's where you come in.

Of course, there are some fields of sales in which the primary focus may well be on first-time buyers; insurance comes to mind. Here, too, however, it is a little simplistic to look at the process as simply 'finding the need'. Any good insurance agent can tell you that a major part of his job is *educating* – filling in the knowledge gaps the first-time buyer brings to the table, and then providing the information necessary for that person to make the right choice. This requires no small degree of tact, patience and persistence – all for a considerable time after the need is found. Think about it. If you're a person who 'needs' life insurance, and who does not require any assistance or new information to get to that point, what are you going to do? Call up the life insurance company!

Remember; in dealing with a customer who already uses a competing product or service – as we so often must – we have to remember that the need itself has already been established. It has been so firmly established that the person has opted to take time from a very busy schedule to meet you and discuss it. More sales than you might imagine have been lost because of a sales person's inability to grasp that the focus with the 'educated' customer must be on how to identify and meet new requirements that the current product or service is *not* meeting.

Try to keep things in perspective here. No one is suggesting you should not talk up your products – and vigorously! It's all a question of how. Prattling on about how wonderful Brand Y widgets are – when compared to no widgets – is suicidal. Discussing the specific ways

Brand Y widgets will deliver more, perform better or make for a more attractive budget than Brand X is the way you will make the sale. Look at each lead as a sales relationship – and remember that relationships take time to develop.

Technique 6:
Converting the Leads that 'Fall into Your Lap'

It's a dream come true. You're at work minding your own business when suddenly someone calls, apparently out of the blue, and virtually asks you for business. Wow!

I know what the first temptation is. You want to close the sale. Life is tough enough; you spend all day building, establishing, persuading. Now along comes the sale you deserve, and you're certainly not going to let it slip through your fingers. So you start to move in.

Don't.

It will take some discipline. (Let's be honest; it will take a lot of discipline.) But if you really want to move the lead from other end of the receiver on to your commission cheque, I promise you that the surest way to do it is to take a deep breath, count to three, and follow a few simple steps.

1. Back off and establish some kind of relationship. If this really is someone you've never spoken to before, you don't know whether or not a brusque, let's-get-down-to-business, of-course-we-can-solve-your-problem approach is going to work. It may backfire spectacularly, and often has. So exchange a few pleasantries; get a feeling for the kind of person you're talking to.

2. Find out what's going on. Say, 'I'm really glad you got in touch with me; listen, do you mind if I ask what prompted your call?' This is very important! You have to know exactly what you're dealing with; no sale exists in a vacuum. Things may not be what they seem! Sometimes people call, sound as though they're ready to sign on, but really need generous amounts of tender loving care. Establish your surroundings; get the information. Don't succumb to the temptation to sell – it may be too early.

3. Ask to set up an appointment. Yes, even if the person tries to close the sale himself on the phone. (Unless, of course, you're involved with telesales.) You need to establish a personal bond.

Don't assume you've got a 'sure thing'. Sales is a numbers game; your objective is to turn the odds in your favour in as many different ways, and on as many different occasions, as humanly possible. If you do that over the long haul, it will pay off handsomely.

Technique 7:
Knowing How to Make Your Product or Service Fit Somewhere Else

How can you adapt an existing product or service to satisfy a prospect?

In my seminars, I talk a lot about product/service 'malleability', by which I mean 'flexibility' or 'capacity for being adapted'.

Dentists use gold and silver for fillings because of the malleability of those metals; they are easily manipulated, and provide a complete, secure fit over and within a cavity. Along the same lines, you might want to think about the ways your product or service can be adjusted or customised for new prospects to meet specific requirements.

Let's take a look at a simple example. Suppose you're in the paper-clip business. How many ways do you think you could use paper clips? Obviously, you can think of a paper clip as a small metal item used to fasten sheets of paper together. But if you stop and think about it for a moment, you'll realise that people use paper clips for all kinds of different purposes. Some people use them to clean out hard-to-reach places on office equipment;

some people use them to mend spectacles; some people make decorative chains out of them. I personally have used (with great care!) two paper clips as a tiny clamp to extract a stubborn disk that would not eject from my computer's drive.

There are probably a hundred different uses for a paper clip apart from holding sheets of paper together. Are there a hundred different uses for your product or service that you may not have considered? Before you discuss this possibility, keep in mind that you don't need a hundred to boost your sales. You just need one.

Baking powder is for cooking, right? Well, it can be . . . but it can also be used to cure indigestion.

We all know how awful tannin stains look on china and teaspoons. But did you know that these stains can be removed using Steradent, the well-known denture cleaner? Or that some people use lemonade to prolong the life of cut flowers or that ladies tights can be used in an emergency to fix the fan-belt of your car?

That's product malleability.

Does what you sell work in only one way? Or can you adjust it? Can you make it serve some new purpose or function? Can you present it in a different light, or to a different group of people? The key lies in opening your own mind to new possibilities – then following through.

That is not to say that you have to become a successful inventor to make this principle work for you. Keep it simple to begin with. You can start with just one variation. If it's a winner, you may well find that it can change not only your career in sales – but perhaps also change the business you work for!

Technique 8:
Pretending You're
a Consultant
(Because You Are)

Treat all your sales work as a consulting assignment.

Many years ago, I found myself stuck while working with a new prospect. I was trying to develop a programme for him, and things simply weren't working out.

So this is what I did. I said, 'Charlie, rather than go any further with this, let me think about what we've talked about here and come back next week with a couple of ideas. Then, if you like them, we can continue our discussion.' He agreed to that; I eventually closed the sale.

It was shortly after that meeting that I realised what I had done. I had taken the same approach I would normally take with a client who was simply asking for an evaluation of the problems on his firm's sales staff. I had taken the 'sell' sign down for a moment and come to grips with the fact that, since I did not yet have an adequate assessment of the prospect's problems, *I could not offer him a solution.*

There's a catch to selling from the point of view of the

consultant: you have to be willing to stop and think once in a while.

The best sales people are professional problem solvers. If you sell cars, then you should consider yourself in the business of solving transport problems. If you sell photocopiers, then you should consider yourself in the business of solving photocopying problems. If you sell cellular phones, then you should consider yourself in the business of solving communication problems. But you have to know and understand the problem first, before you can try to solve it. You have to be willing to walk in the door without any preconceived notions as to how best to solve the problems identified.

For many sales people, the consulting principle can be put on an even simpler footing. If you sell to other companies, you should consider yourself in the business of solving *profitability* problems. That's the key concern you will ultimately be addressing: how to increase profitability. Everything you do, every proposal you offer, every product or programme you put forward, should lead eventually to the goal of your client's firm increasing its level of profitability. Measure your goals and approaches against this standard, and you will have gone a long way towards achieving sales success.

If you're *not* interested in helping people to solve problems, then I respectfully suggest that you're not in the right business. If you can't break everything you do down into something that helps another person to reach an important goal, you will either base your sales on manipulating others or fail to persuade prospects that you are offering anything of value. Either path leads inexorably to burn-out and/or constant rejection. You definitely don't need that.

The dictionary defines 'consult' as 'to seek advice, information, or guidance from'. To me, this definition pinpoints exactly the relationship between a qualified prospect and a professional salesperson. You as a salesperson are there to advise the prospect of the ways you can help to solve existing problems; to provide all necessary information relative to solving those problems; and to provide the guidance that will result in a harmonious professional association.

Act like a consultant . . . because that's really what you are!

Technique 9:
Asking for the Next Appointment While You're on the First Visit

This is perhaps the easiest piece of advice to follow in this book. Yet it is also a step that sales people routinely ignore. Many are even afraid to take it once it is highlighted as a key to success!

A young sales person once said to me, 'Steve, that's not my place. I'm in the prospect's office. He's showing me a courtesy by seeing me in the first place. If I'm going to go back there for a second visit, the prospect should ask me.'

Rubbish!

You initiated the contact in the first place. You have made it clear at every point in the process that your objective is to help the prospect. You have demonstrated that you are interested primarily in solving a problem for him. Why on earth shouldn't you ask the prospect for the next appointment so you can show how you would implement the solution?

This point is – to me, at any rate – so basic that it requires little argument in its favour. Yet it never ceases to amaze me that I receive bewildered looks when I suggest it to sales people. Here are some actual answers I've received from sales people in response to the suggestion that they set up their next appointment during the first visit.

'I can't ask for the appointment; I don't know when I'll be back in the area.'

'I can't ask for the appointment; I don't know how long it will take me to write the proposal.'

'I can't ask for the appointment; I don't have a quote ready for the prospect yet.'

'I can't ask for the appointment; he may not want to give it to me.'

These are genuine sales people talking! Can you believe it?

If you have to make a rough guess at the amount of time it will take you to pull a quote together or coordinate with one of your team members, then *guess!* What's the worst thing that could happen? You may have to telephone the prospect's office to rearrange the appointment. Big deal.

You didn't set up the initial appointment for the good of your health. You did it because you had an objective: helping to solve the prospect's problem with your product or service. You still have that objective at the conclusion of your initial visit; therefore it is appropriate for you to ask to move the process along to the next stage before the meeting adjourns.

Unless you receive a firm, unequivocal 'no' at the first meeting, there will always be a next stage to talk about. And the best possible time to set the appointment for discussing that next stage is right then. You're both sitting there at the same time. You both have your diaries within reach. You both have pens or pencils handy. What better time to set up your next meeting? What on earth would induce you to leave that room without knowing when you will next meet the person?

'Okay, Mr Jones; I think we've gone about as far with this as we can today. What I'd like to do is meet you in a couple of weeks' time to show you exactly what we can do for your company. How about Friday the fifteenth?'

Listen for the response. (There has to be a response of some kind!) Then work from there with the information you receive.

Technique 10:
Taking Notes

Taking notes during your meeting with the prospect can be one of your most powerful sales tools.

Taking notes will reinforce, both for you and the prospect, the reason you turned up in the first place: to learn more about the prospect's problems.

Taking notes helps you to listen. There's something about having an empty sheet of paper in front of you that really tunes you in to what is being said, and makes it more difficult for you to miss important points.

Taking notes puts you in a position of authority and control. Believe me, during the opening 20 minutes of most first-time sales visits, you need all the help you can get.

Taking notes strengthens your analytical abilities. If you write down notes during your interview, you're using three senses: touch (that is, your hand, which is doing the writing), hearing (what you have to do to listen to the prospect) and sight (to see what you've written). My experience has been that by approaching a problem through tactile, visual and aural stimuli, you're usually in a much better position to come up with a solution.

Taking notes will encourage the prospect to open up. You may doubt this, but don't knock it until you've tried it. Every time I conduct a seminar, I get further proof of how effective the simple act of writing something down (in this case, on a flipchart, blackboard or overhead projector) can be in encouraging communication. When I simply stand in front of an audience and ask, 'What was good about the presentation we just heard?', nothing happens. When I stand in front of an audience and write 'GOOD POINTS IN PRESENTATION' across the top, then ask for suggestions – wham! The room comes alive!

Taking notes sends strong positive signals to the prospect, and you can never do that too much. When the prospect says, 'I have 500 trucks, each of which holds 75 widgets, making deliveries 320 days a year', and then looks over and sees that you've written '500 × 75 widgets × 320 days/yr', guess what? You've scored! You care! You're listening!

I'd suggest you use a notebook with a hard cardboard backing. It needs to be stiff enough for you to be able to write while it's on your lap. Keep your notes clean and brief, remember that they should be legible to both you and the prospect at all times. Where appropriate, draw oversized diagrams in your notes to emphasise a point you're making verbally – and show your diagrams to the prospect.

Technique 11:
Creating a Plan With Each New Prospect

I go through a little monologue each time I meet a new prospect. I say, 'Here's someone new. Here's someone I've never met before. What am I going to do that will be a little different with this person?'

It may be routine for you, but the prospect you're dealing with has never gone through the sales cycle with you before. One of the best ways I know to combat that 'here I go again' sensation (and that's a danger for even the very best sales people) is to produce a customised, written plan for your prospect. This should be based on the material you gather in your notes during the first and subsequent meetings.

After a while, you become familiar with certain objections or problems. And it's all too easy to categorise your prospect. 'I know that one; that's just like the problem the manager at ABC Company had.' Well, it is and it isn't. It is not like the ABC problem in that the person who just outlined it has nothing to do with ABC Company, and probably faces a number of different challenges related to the problem he has just brought up.

A prospect who offers up an objection is really making

a gesture of good faith. That may sound a little bizarre, but it's true. By taking the time to share a concern or problem with you, your prospect is passing along important information, key facts on the way your product or service needs to be adapted. Listening is the first part of the secret – and identifying the mutually accepted solutions is the second part.

Find out what those challenges are, being sure to be aware of the unique circumstances or background your prospect may face. Then commit the solutions to paper, working with your prospect to determine the outline of the plan that will make the most sense in the current situation.

If you go to the doctor because you have a stomach ache, you don't care if he's seen three thousand other people with stomach aches over the course of his long and illustrious career. The last thing you want is for him to rush into the room, look you up and down, mumble some technical phrase you've never heard before, and scratch something on a prescription pad before hustling away again.

No. You want him to ask how you feel, how long you've felt that way, whether you've ever felt that way before, exactly where it hurts, what medicines you may be allergic to, and any other pertinent questions. If a doctor does all that, you're likely to be a better patient – and you'll probably have a better attitude about coming to see him next time.

You're the doctor. It doesn't matter how many patients you've seen before. This one is the only one you're seeing now. Like the best doctors, you should make an effort to include the patient in your diagnosis and treatment. Doing so not only makes for a better atmosphere for you to conduct your work in, it also increases the likelihood that your patient will have the positive attitude that is really the driving force behind so many dramatic recoveries!

Technique 12:
Asking for Referrals

My favourite story about referrals has to do with a very successful salesperson I know named Bill. Every year he takes a holiday in some exotic location like Fiji or the Caribbean or Hawaii. Often, thse holidays come as a result of company bonuses for his performance or industry awards. So about once a year, this agent sends a letter to his customers and qualified prospects announcing his return from Paradise, where he received the XYZ Award for Outstanding Salesmanship. The purpose of the letter is to thank the salesperson's clients for their business, and to make it perfectly clear that the only way the salesperson has been able to attain his goals is by helping customers attain theirs.

At the end of the letter is a paragraph that runs something like this: 'As you know, my business depends on referrals. I would very much appreciate it if you take a moment now to jot down the names and phone numbers of three or four people in your industry who you feel might benefit from talking to me. Of course, if you do not wish me to use your name when contacting these people, all you have to do is indicate this in the space I've provided below. Again, thank you for your business, and here's to continuing success for both of us.'

Call me crazy. But I have a feeling there may be some cause-and-effect connection between letters like that and all those expensive holidays and impressive sales awards.

Let's play a little multiplication game. Suppose five people give you five referrals each, to make a total of 25. And suppose that, of those new referrals, 60 per cent turn around and give you 5 referrals, too. That's 15 times 5, or 75 new prospects. Now, if of those 75, 60 per cent can give you 5 referrals each . . . you get the picture. If you're out to build your client base (and why wouldn't you be?), you'll have trouble finding a better place to start asking for referrals.

Referrals are the lifeblood of a successful career in sales. And yet sales people are usually terrified to ask for them.

Often, they feel it will somehow threaten the relationship they've built up with a customer to ask if there are other associates of that customer who might benefit from their product or service. Perhaps the customer really doesn't like using the product or service after all – and asking for a referral will only intensify that feeling or bring it to the surface.

Conservatism is one thing. Paranoia is another.

You should be able to tell without too much difficulty whether or not you have a satisfied customer or an enthusiastic prospect. If you do, what that really means is that you have established the foundations of a *productive, mutually beneficial relationship*. Why on earth wouldn't your customer want to share that kind of relationship with his friends and associates? Assuming there is no competitive or other business conflict involved, there is every reason in the world to expect a referral – and one passed along happily and enthusiastically.

How can you make referrals work for you? Let's say your goal is to get five new prospects for the week. Carry with you at all times a packet of index cards. At the end of a meeting with one of your customers or a good quality prospect, simply say something like this.

> *'Mr Jones, I'm willing to bet there are people in your (industry, area, related businesses) who could benefit from my talking to them about this (product/service).'*

As you say this, you take out five index cards. Hold them in your hand. Let the prospect or customer see that there are five of them there. Then say,

> *'Do you know of five people I could talk to?'*

Help him or her along. It will be easier than you think; the fact that there are five separate index cards will make the task comprehensible and immediate. Your confident, professional attitude will guarantee that your request will not be seen as inappropriate.

Put the cards in a row on the desk as you fill them in, writing names only. Then after you have identified the five referrals by name, go back and ask for the company affiliations, addresses or other contact infor-mation. You do this because you want to make the first and most important job, identifying the people you can talk to, as easy as possible.

I know of one salesperson who will actually ask his contact at this point, 'Frank, how would you feel about calling these people for me?' Of course, the contact says 'no' and says the salesperson should make the call – and then the salesperson says, 'Yes, you're right, I probably should call them. You don't mind if I use your name, I hope?' He has never yet been turned down on the second question – which was the one he wanted a 'yes' answer to in the first place.

That's an aggressive approach, and it's not one I'm sure I'd recommend to all sales people. But it certainly illustrates the point that you can profit enormously when it comes to referrals by taking the initiative and asking for what you want!

Technique 13:
Showing Enthusiasm

No, this doesn't mean embracing your prospect, pumping his arm up and down 20 times every time you shake hands with him, or issuing endless implausible compliments about dress or appearance.

There is a difference between enthusiasm and poorly disguised panic. Enthusiasm builds bridges. Panic tears them down.

A sales meeting is like any other interaction. It takes a certain amount of time to get off the ground. If you understand the dynamics that are at work when you first come into contact with a prospect, you will go a long way towards understanding how enthusiasm must be conveyed as the relationship progresses.

When people meet someone new, they pass through a number of stages. There is among human beings a certain 'putting feelers out' process, an introductory stage. You cannot say convincingly at this stage all that you might want to about solving the prospect's problem, because the two of you don't know each other well enough yet. The prospect – along with most of the rest of the adult members of our species – will require a certain 'choosing' time before entering a socialisation stage with another person. So the best way to show enthusiasm in the very early part of the meeting is to underplay it. Confident bearing; good eye contact (but not to such a degree that it could be confused with staring): a firm handshake; predictable, smooth movements as you walk from one point to another; these are the keys to communicating your excitement about the new relationship you're trying to build.

Only you can tell when the prospect enters the second stage of socialisation, but rest assured that the change will be noticeable. It will be marked by a more relaxed, open approach, often reflected in less constricted body language. What you are looking for is the point at which the prospect listens, not because he has agreed to do so, but because he wants to. Once you see that shift take place – and it may be during the first visit or during a subsequent one – you can change the 'grammar' of your presentation.

You may decide to use your hands more in gesturing, or to use the prospect's preferred form of address ('Mr Powers' or 'Bill') somewhat more frequently. You might even feel comfortable using less formal phrasings and word choices: 'Take a look for yourself!', 'How about that?', 'And I'll tell you what we did.'

Make an effort to avoid repetitive, mechanical gestures or responses. This is exactly what constitutes an unspontaneous, unenthusiastic meeting. If *your* conversational partner insisted on constantly nodding his head up and down, with little real regard for what you had to say, how would you feel?

These are general guidelines; your individual interactions with prospects will vary, because prospects themselves will vary. The point is, bolstering your presentation with appropriate enthusiasm (especially on the second and subsequent visits) is an essential part of good salesmanship.

Technique 14:
Giving Yourself Appropriate Credit

Talk about yourself – but be humble.

The two instructions are not mutually exclusive. I want you to learn how to do both. There's nothing wrong with walking into the prospect's office and talking with confidence and pride about what you do. Too many sales people can't seem to grasp that this is the reason they arrive in the first place! The only trap to watch out for is that of appearing arrogant. Fortunately, that's easy to avoid.

When you walk in to meet the prospect, you will want to convey success, confidence and flexibility. That's not arrogance. That's professionalism, and you should be proud of it. You should be able to talk, in detail, about the things that make you successful.

I am not suggesting you play one-up with the prospect by boasting about how great your kids look, how good your golf game is, or how much money you make. That's a game you can't win, no matter how the conversation ends.

What I am suggesting is the aggressive promotion of your ability to succeed at your chosen task, and it requires a good deal of discretion on your part. You have to learn how to read the situation. You have to know when to step back. You have to know that what works for Prospect A in one situation may not work at all with Prospect B in another situation. What I'm suggesting carries the very real risk that, if you don't read the signals correctly, you may overwhelm your prospect. But it's still worth thinking about, because far too many sales people *underwhelm* the prospect, and that's just as dangerous. At least with my way, you know there's no way you're going to fade into the anonymous parade of mediocre sales people most decision makers have to face!

Yes. There is a definite risk here. But in my view, it's a risk worth taking.

Try it with the next prospect you see.

'Mr Jones, I am really glad to see you. This has been a really big week for us – we just completed the XYZ project. Let me tell you about it.'

Wow! Here's a person who makes things happen!

In an earlier chapter, we used a doctor/patient analogy. I'm going to revise it a little bit to make a different point here.

This time, suppose you walk into the doctor's surgery and the minute the doctor walks in the door, you notice that he looks more ill than you do. He's wheezing and coughing and holding a stubby, half-smoked cigarette between his fingers. He totters a little bit as he walks. His eyes are yellowish. He has trouble focusing on things.

Is this the man who's going to solve your health problem?

For many professionals, there are two kinds of people: those who add value to whatever they touch, and those who cause the value of everything they touch to decline. Prove that you fall into that first category. Show your value! Demonstrate it! Broadcast it! Shout it from the rooftops! As long as you do so without affecting an air of superiority, your self-promotion will be perceived as security. Not arrogance, but admirable, enthusiastic, security in your own mission and your ability to carry it out.

Technique 15:
Telling the Truth
(It's Easier to Remember)

Someone did a study at a university recently on the issue of exactly how many 'white lies' the average person tells during the course of a day. Can you guess the results?

The answer came out to be approximately 200.

That's a lot of lying! And that's only the average. But let's be clear about what the researchers were looking for. When they went out looking for 'white lies', they were looking for all the times someone said to someone else, 'I'm glad you could come today,' when in fact the person wasn't all that glad. Those kinds of falsehoods – which we could also classify as harmless social convention – aren't what I'm talking about when I advise you to tell the truth to your client.

Sales people are relationship-orientated. They build relationships on trust and personal contact, and they live and die on the strength of those relationships. That this is the case serves as a convincing argument *for* telling the occasional 'white social lie' and *against* telling any other kind of lie. Let's look at a couple of examples.

'This is a lovely office. I wish I worked in a place like this.' (Actually, the office you work in easily outshines the prospect's.)

No big deal. Some sales people find it easier to make a contact with the prospect by finding something like this to comment on as they're breaking the ice. What's the problem if there's a slight exaggeration on a point like this? Even if the prospect should somehow learn the terrible truth that you work in a spectacular office, is there any real disadvantage to such a statement made tactfully, and without any overbearing flourishes? No.

'And about the delivery time you're asking for. I don't think we should have any problem meeting that, though I will have to clear it with the technical people after we sort out the paperwork today.' (Actually, you know full well that you will miss the prospect's requested date by two weeks no matter what you say to the people in production.)

Red light! You are attempting to build a new relationship with a potential customer by deliberately misrepresenting your ability to solve his problem to his satisfaction. When things go wrong later on – and nine times out of ten in this situation, they will – the prospect is not going to remember the little disclaimer you slid in about running things by the technical people. He's going to remember that you said you could deliver the product on the first, and it didn't make it into the warehouse until the fifteenth. At that stage, you will no longer be regarded as a problem solver. You will be regarded as a problem: a salesperson who promises more than can be delivered. This is not the stuff of which repeat sales are made.

If you need further convincing, consider this. Once you make a habit of simply telling everyone what they want to hear, you're eventually going to run into a serious problem: you won't be able to keep your story straight. You'll be dealing with 15 different clients, each of whom has received 15 different, customised pie-in-the-sky assurances. It will only be a matter of time until you become hopelessly muddled . . . and slip up disastrously.

Don't risk it. Tell the truth; it's easier to remember.

Technique 16:
Selling Yourself on Yourself

The following are some ideas you can use to motivate yourself. Use them!

Don't listen to the radio during your morning commute. Radio programmes are filled with lots of depressing news that you won't be able to do anything about anyway. You'll hear soon enough about any news of consequence; reserve the morning for yourself. Buy some motivational tapes and make a habit of using the drive (or ride) in to work as a time for positive messages and clear-headed, sober assessments of the day ahead. I know of one salesperson so committed to this principle that he honestly does not know whether or not the radio in his car works on all channels!

Be specific with your goals – and your rewards. Perhaps your dream is to own a Lamborghini. Fine. Put a photo of one on your desk or on your refrigerator at home. Or perhaps you look at things a bit more analytically: your goal is to close six new sales over the next month. Take a piece of paper and commit yourself to the goal by writing it down. This will make your aims more tangible and increase the likelihood that they will be attained.

Get positive reinforcement. I think it's fascinating how many successful sales 'teams' there are – two individuals who sell completely independently, but who rely on each other for constant support, advice and constructive criticism. For most of us, this really is a far better alternative than going it alone; if you can establish such a relationship in your current work environment, give it a try and see what happens.

Get outside. Yes, you do need a lunch break. No, you shouldn't work through the lunch hour. (My studies on this with sales people lead me to believe that those who make a point of putting work aside for an hour and getting outside in the fresh air are actually *more* productive in terms of sales volume than those eager beavers who don't know when to stop.)

Leave yourself notes. 'I can do it.' 'Most of the things I worry about never happen.' 'I have solved the problems of over 500 customers.' Try to leave them on your desk Friday afternoon; you'll probably forget about it until Monday morning, when it will be a pleasant surprise.

Keep things in perspective. At my office, we make a habit of issuing a humorous reminder to each other: 'It's not brain surgery.' It isn't! Missed calls, forgotten deadlines, problems with customers . . . challenging as it all can be, it really isn't the end of the world. Sometimes things seem larger than they are. Try to keep that in mind as the day progresses. (For me, this lesson is particularly important between about two and four in the afternoon; that's when the day really *can* start to seem like an unending series of brain surgery projects. Is there a similar time for you? If so, that's when you should be sure to give yourself a break!)

Technique 17:
Starting Early

Did you know that you can often get past the 'secretary trap' by making your important cold calls before 9.00am? A lot of decision makers are given to arriving at the office before the rest of the crowd shows up, and they might just pick up their own phone if you call them then.

That's one obvious advantage to getting an early start on the day. There are any number of others. For one thing, you won't be disturbed by the normal crisis mentality that seems to set in around 9.01. For another, you'll be able to do your relaxing, newspaper-shuffling, and paperwork-managing at some time other than the peak contact hours during the business day. That's an advantage that can add up in a hurry. As I'm fond of pointing out, a sales person is similar to a retail outlet in that location is often the key requirement for success – except that your location is the number of people you talk to during the day.

There's more. My guess is that you'll find your journey to work a great deal easier if you make an earlier start in the morning. That may seem like a minor consideration – until you realise how important attitude is in sales work. In so many big cities these days, you spend an hour simply getting from point A to point B in the morning. That's a lot of time, but the key consideration is really the aggravation you're likely to run into during that much 'driving time' (or train or bus time, for that matter). If you spend up to 60 minutes of every morning swearing at people and scowling at red lights that seem designed to slow you down, you will probably find that your first few calls of the day are less than productive. You'll lose your edge before you talk to even a single potential customer – and that's a shame.

Finally, let me add an important observation, based on my experiences and those of many of the successful sales people I've worked with: the day really does seem to go better if you take a couple of moments of quiet time for yourself before charging into the fray. There's something very hard on the system about bursting through the door of your office at 8.59 and having to plunge in cold, no matter what that entails. I have a strong feeling that sales people who do this are costing themselves sales; the first few calls they make in the morning are 'warm-ups', whether they like it or not. Of course, the best of all possible worlds would be to show up for work early enough to have a little time to yourself, and then do some role-playing with a colleague to make sure the warm-up calls aren't directed at live prospects.

Technique 18:
Reading Industry Publications (Yours and Your Clients')

What kind of people read *The Structural Engineer?* How about *The Bookseller?* What audience do you expect would subscribe to *Media Week?* Or to *The Stage?*

You may not find them on a lot of news-stands, but these publications, and hundreds more like them, may be the most important magazines you can get your hands on. The industry or industries you work in almost certainly have some sort of trade journal or magazine read by just about everyone of any consequence within the field. You can put yourself at a distinct competitive advantage over many sales people by becoming familiar with these publications. Use them to keep abreast of industry trends. You should understand and be able to adapt to the business environment faced by your customers.

Subscriptions tend to be expensive, but you may be able to find back issues of the magazine or journal you're looking for in any large library.

You will probably find that you can get a much better understanding of the technical jargon employed in your target group by reading the articles in trade and professional magazines. Of course, you may have some trouble with a few of the denser articles aimed at specialised groups within an industry, but you're much better off puzzling things out on paper now than nodding your head vacantly when the terms are rattled off later!

The 'who's who' or 'on the move' sections of these publications can be a particularly fertile source of sales leads. In these columns, you will find the names and company affiliations of people who have recently been promoted or taken on by a given company. Who wouldn't be flattered by a brief note of congratulations on having appeared in such a column – followed up by a phone call a few days later to talk about your company's product or service?

You might even decide to keep a running file on references to the various companies or individuals appearing in trade magazines. This can help to break the ice when meeting a new prospect. For my part, I can tell you that I'd much prefer being able to cite three interesting points about a prospect culled from the pages of a trade magazine than be forced to talk for 20 minutes about the weather or how attractive the prospect's children are!

Technique 19:
Supporting Your Visit the Next Day

Telephone or write to your prospect the day after your visit. The vast majority of sales people *mean* to do this but never actually get around to it. I strongly suggest that you build these contacts into your daily schedule ... so you can be certain to follow up during that crucial period after the meeting.

Don't try to initiate contact any later than one day after the visit to the prospect; the whole point of this 'supporting' manoeuvre is to re-establish your presence and your commitment to solving the prospect's problems. Do so tactfully and without being overbearing.

This is how it might sound in a telephone call.

'Mr Smith, this Mary Powers from InfoWorld Ltd. I wanted to take a minute to thank you for sparing the time to see me yesterday. I thought the meeting went well. How did you feel about it?'

I mention the phone contact first because it seems to be the most likely means of communication for such a message in today's sales environment. I should point out, though, that an old-fashioned typed or printed letter on company stationery can win a good deal of positive attention. It's less likely to happen, of course, because time is at such a premium these days (and because so many sales people honestly don't like to write letters). But that can work in your favour: your courteous, neat, well-written letter will stand alone.

Don't drone on and on in this piece of correspondence. The letter you send should be *very* brief!

Take a look at the following model; your letter should resemble it fairly closely.

---

24 April 1992

Dear Mr Smith

I just wanted to drop a line to thank you for making time in your busy schedule to meet me yesterday.

I found the ideas we exchanged were very exciting, and I think you'll agree that there is the potential for a mutually beneficial relationship between your firm and ours.

Mr Smith, I hope you will feel free to call me if there are any questions or problems I can help you to resolve.

Yours sincerely,

Mary Powers
Mary Powers

Try it. What you'll find is that contacting the prospect in this way is an excellent means of winning involvement and interest – and to reassert your credentials as a problem solver.

Warning: You can undo a lot of your hard work if you succumb to the temptation of trying to close the sale during your 'support' contact with the prospect. Keep to your cycle; use the phone call or letter to reinforce the points you felt were strongest about the meeting. Don't press the prospect or change the ground rules that have been established.

Technique 20:
Giving Speeches to Business and Civic Groups

Public speaking rates as one of the most commonly shared fears human beings have. Yet I'm going to suggest that you take time to develop your skills as a speaker and get out and share your (unparallelled!) expertise in your field with audiences – and not just audiences of people in your industry. Just about any audience, believe it or not, will do the trick.

There is a double-edged sword at work here. First, you will benefit tremendously from the boost in confidence you receive from being treated as an expert in your field. By the way, if you don't consider yourself an expert in your field, you shouldn't be selling in it. Your customers are certainly counting on your expertise.

Think about it. You know your subject. You talk about it all day long. Once you can make the minor adjustment of being able to give a lecture about what you do, you'll be a lecturer. Do several lectures and you will become a 'well-known lecturer', or an 'established lecturer'. And deservedly so!

So the first benefit is reinforcement. You may know intellectually that you and your firm possess everything necessary to solve problems A, B and C, but believe me, you will receive an extraordinary emotional charge from actually getting up on stage and talking about A, B and C to a group of willing listeners. If you don't think that that affirmation will carry over positively into the way you deal with prospects, my guess is that you haven't been in sales very long.

The second benefit is even more remarkable. Studies have shown that when sales people and consultants give speeches, an average of one out of every ten audience members will seek out the speaker afterwards to ask about his or her services. What this really means is that *10 per cent* of any given audience you talk to will end up *qualifying itself* – and entering your prospect cycle. Who knows what might happen if you actually took the initiative to shake some hands and pass out business cards during intervals and at the event's conclusion?

It may take some effort on your part to get to the point where you feel comfortable addressing a group, but I assure you the effort will be worth it. Remember that even the most accomplished professional speakers complain of stage fright. Your goal should not be to get every butterfly out of your stomach, but to learn to make the adrenalin work for you.

Where do you go to give the speech? Well, outside the channels that may exist in your industry (such as addressing a trade conference or taking part in an annual convention), consider contacting your Chamber of Commerce about local Round Tables. Other possibilities include your area's Rotary Club, local branch of a trade association, or any group that seems relevant to the economy of your community or tied in somehow to what you do.

Go to the club or organisation you've targeted, state your case, and see what happens. More often than not, they'll be glad to work you into the schedule.

So: ask yourself. What have you got to lose? Absolutely nothing! If it doesn't work out, at least you've made an effort – and got your name out in front of that many more potential prospects. Give public speaking a try. More than one sales person has benefited tremendously from taking this route!

Technique 21:
Passing the Word When the Opportunity is Appropriate

What goes around, comes around.

This is a hard one for a lot of sales people to relate to, but is nevertheless a vitally important point.

Maintaining a can-do attitude where your own efforts are concerned is easy enough. But why on earth should you make an effort to help someone else out if you don't have to – if there seems to be no logical way for that person to help you out somewhere down the line in *your* career?

The answer is complicated. Perhaps the best illustration I can give is to offer an example from the world of golf.

Have you ever noticed that after teeing off, a golfer will often joke around a little bit with his opponent on the other team? That's a little odd, isn't it? Considering that these are professional competitors dealing with members of the opposition, you'd expect a more stern uncompromising attitude. But there they are, joking, nodding, smiling at one another.

You usually can't hear what they're saying. Interestingly enough, it turns out that, both on the course, and in their other contacts, opposing players often discuss some aspect of the game they play for a living. Of course, they're not giving away important strategy points that would give any competitive advantage in the game at hand. But they are often discussing points of interest that concern their own development as golfers. Even though they may be on opposite teams, two golfers, for instance, will often discuss the irregularities of the surface on a given course, or pass on information on how to tackle a course in another area that is particularly windy or wet.

They pass on these facts not because they do not see each other as competitors (they do!), but because they also see each other as colleagues – and it's not a bad idea to be known as the type of person who likes to help out a colleague. You might get your own hot tip on how to approach that new course or play in extremely dry dusty conditions! You don't know you're going to get such a tip, but because you're 'part of the grapevine', you'll certainly get whatever is circulating.

Let me mention here before I'm inundated with letters from golfing enthusiasts about this that I'm talking about general trends among most golfers. You do find the occasional hard-nosed type who refuses to share a kind word with an opposing player, but that's the exception, not the rule. Many of these tight-lipped players are new to the game and concentrating on trying to learn the ropes and remain in the major championships, and not on contributing to 'the grapevine' or the collection of accepted, widely circulated strategies currently influencing decisions in golfing circles.

Is there a grapevine in your field? If so, do you contribute to it? Do you share insights, leads and contacts with others where appropriate, even though you cannot see any immediate benefit in doing so? There are hundreds, probably thousands of stories of strange, off-the-wall referrals generated 'through the grapevine' that resulted in sales. To get your share, you'll need to develop a reputation as a person who contributes to that common pool of resources, tips, and openings.

Pass the word when you have the opportunity. It's a wise investment – one I've never heard any sales person regret making.

Technique 22:
Taking Responsibility For Presentations that Go Haywire

Assuming personal responsibility for the sale is a remarkably effective sales tool. It works so well that, if you're like me, the first time you hear about the technique, you'll probably wonder why on earth you didn't incorporate it into your sales routine long ago.

To start with, you have to be utterly, completely convinced in your own heart that you can offer your prospect the best possible solution to his problem. If that confidence isn't there, the technique I'm about to describe simply won't work. If the prospect (or anyone else) asks you to talk about your firm, you have to be able to reply with sincerity that you work for a one-of-a-kind, customer-first company and are proud to do so.

When you're on a sales visit, and you come to the closing stage, you simply ask the prospect when the best time would be for the product to be delivered or the service to start. One of two things will happen. Either the prospect will answer your question receptively – and thereby become a customer – or the prospect will back off and say no. If you find yourself facing the second scenario, you take responsibility.

At this point, the sales people I know who use this technique are genuinely taken aback – even shocked. And it's no act. They believe in their company so completely, and know so much about the prospect by this stage of the game, that they are legitimately concerned to see any evidence of a negative response to the proposal they've made. And they state that concern in no uncertain terms. You can, too.

Here's what you say:

> *'Mr Jones, I'm really not sure what to say. I am so convinced that we have the best service, the best pricing, the best customisation, and the best reputation of any firm in our industry that I can think of only one reason for you not to sign up with us. And that's that I must have done something terribly wrong just now in giving my presentation. So I'm going to ask you to give me a hand, Mr Jones, and tell me where I went off course. Because, to be quite frank, I know this service is right for you, and I'd really hate to have made a mistake like that.'*

What do you think you'll hear in response? One thing's certain. It's not going to be easy for the prospect to come back with a run-of-the-mill brush-off like, 'It's just not up our street, Maureen.' No, if you're Mr Jones, you probably respect the person who has had the courage to say that to you and who believes strongly in the service you're looking at. You're going to pass on information – information on exactly what the problem is with your firm's signing up.

The common response you'll hear after you take responsibility for the inital 'no' will sound something like this: 'No, no, no, Maureen, it has nothing to do with you. It's at our end.' And the prospect can then be expected to go into detail about the remaining obstacles. Then you have the facts you need to continue through the cycle.

Let me repeat: this can be a startlingly effective technique, but it requires abosolute faith on your part that you can, in fact, deliver on your promises. There is another catch, as well: you have to be willing to put aside the common fixation with 'being right' that we all share to a degree.

But when it comes right down to it, would you rather be 'right' – or close a sale?

Technique 23:
Being Honest With Yourself About the Nature of the Firm You Work For

In my speeches and seminars, I often equate business with war, noting that each field of endeavour demands sound planning, has winners and losers, requires ammunition, features a chain of command, and so on. And I always conclude my remarks in this area by pointing out that business does have a few major advantages over war: nobody gets killed, and you can change armies.

Changing armies and the honest self-assessment that is often required to do so are the issues at hand. If you're currently in a work environment that does not meet your personal standards for quality, ethics or orientation towards the customer, you should consider moving on. Too often, sales people will stay with an 'army' that's all wrong for them. The reasons given can be endless – don't have time, don't have the contacts, it's not really that bad here, lack of visibility in the industry – but, in the final analysis, they are all rationalisations, and unconvincing ones at that. There is a danger here, because sometimes sales people, who are a persuasive lot, will often go to great lengths to sell *themselves* on an idea. If that idea doesn't really work, the possibility of denial and self-discipline looms. You may have to be on your guard, and make a special effort to be brutally honest with yourself about the direction both you and your firm are headed in.

Why? Because it's your career on the line. You want to work towards developing productive, mutually beneficial relationships with all the people you encounter on a professional level. If you find that your sales work now is not doing that for you – if you find that, to the contrary, you are leaving a trail of angry former customers in your wake – you are asking for trouble.

Some sales people try to play games with themselves. They try to rationalise a situation that is inherently manipulative or abusive and see it as something it isn't and will never be. Don't be one of them. Don't set yourself up for a fall.

You have to feel it in your gut; you have to believe in your cause. You have to know in the marrow of your bones that all your efforts are in line with your value system, and that this system encourages only productive, beneficial-for-both-sides interactions. However you identify your goals, you must be certain that it is right for you to pursue them in this way. You must know instinctively the benefit people will derive from working with you, and you must believe in your heart that all your company's efforts are for the best. Otherwise you may find that you have some difficulty succeeding.

Technique 24:
Telling Everyone You Meet Who You Work For and What You Sell

Why not?

Why not tell your doctor? Your electrician? Your dentist? The taxi driver you used this morning? Your friend at another company? The person you sit next to on a flight? Your hairdresser? Members of the community group or charitable organisation you work with? The man who has the seat next to you at a football match?

Why not make a point of broadcasting your profession to anyone and everyone – with pride? I'm not suggesting you subject everyone you know to a sales pitch, of course. What I am suggesting is that it becomes second nature for you to say, loudly and clearly, to every single person you meet, without exception, that you're a sales person for XYZ Corporation, maker of the finest widgets in the UK. Couple that with a handshake and a confident, look-you-in-the-eye smile, and do you know what? Every so often, someone will say, 'Widgets? You know, we've been thinking about those . . .'

In my opinion, far too many sales people have a pathological aversion to letting people know what they do for a living. The only reason I can see for this is that we often aren't quite as proud of what we do for a living as a brain surgeon might be, or a lawyer, or an editor, or a scientist, or a teacher, or workers in any dozens of other categories who have no difficulty mentioning how they spend the majority of their waking hours.

We *should* be proud of being sales people; I know I am! I know that the economy of the society I live in would not function without people who do what I do for a living, and I know that every transaction I undertake benefits all who are affected by it. Am I proud of that? Of course I am!

You should feel like that about your job, too. If you need to make some changes before you can feel that way, make the changes. Then look people in the eye and tell them what you do and who you do it for. Make it a habit; it may take a little work at first, but eventually you will begin passing on your name, profession and company affiliation almost without thinking. (Here's a helpful hint; current research indicates that a routine you stick with for 21 days will become ingrained, and will become a permanent habit you can incorporate automatically.)

If you have to, start in a small way and work your way up. You might begin by choosing friends or contacts you know well enough to talk to, but who don't yet know what you do for a living. But the easiest route by far is to say what you do for a living and who you do it for *as you are introduced to someone*. It's easier than you think, and it can pay tremendous dividends.

Technique 25:
Keeping Your Sense
of Humour

Let's be honest. It can be tough being a salesperson sometimes. Paradoxically enough, that's exactly why sales work has to be funny now and then.

I can only pass on my own observations about the sales people I've worked with: laughing helps. And not just around the edges. Laughing helps a lot. Sales people depend on a good self-image more than any other professionals I know, and it's awfully hard to keep a good self-image if you take yourself so seriously that you can't back off and laugh about the world once in a while.

Let me sidetrack for a moment. One of the most scathing arguments I know against becoming a salesperson is a very depressing film I saw some years ago called *Salesman*. It's a documentary shot in grainy black-and-white about three travelling sales people. It portrays sales as manipulative, demeaning, dishonest work – work that no thinking, feeling person could ever undertake voluntarily.

I have a real problem with that film, for a couple of reasons. The first is that a great many people who aren't sales people have been exposed to it, and have formed impressions of unrealistic stereotypes about my profession as a result. The second is that most of us who are sales people haven't been exposed to it, and haven't been able to see the debilitating results of consistently bad sales work. This film is convincing proof of how dangerous a salesperson with the wrong attitude can be, both to customers and to the salesperson himself. If you're a salesperson – and especially a salesperson who takes work very seriously – that film will probably have a remarkable effect on you once you see it.

The sales people in this film make just about every mistake in the book, including, but not limited to, failing to establish customer needs, lying to prospects, not listening to prospects, carrying a negative mental attitude, and failing to commit themselves to their own professional development. But there's another error they make that, if rectified, could make all the other problems manageable. *They take the job too seriously and never give themselves a chance to relax.*

It's difficult to attend to these types of problem if they become part of your sales environment, but I can guarantee that there is no way you can approach your sales work the way it *should* be approached, if you can't step back and laugh at yourself once in a while, perferably while at work.

You are too important a resource to let yourself get run down. Take a break. Accept that it *is* all right for you to miss the mark once in a while. Remember that you have to take the long view, and that today's catastrophe usually doesn't mean much tomorrow. This is a message that never really sank in as far as the sales people in the film were concerned. And they paid for it.

Don't let the world at large talk you into thinking you're not in charge of your day, your month, your career. After all, you're the one with the answers; you're the professional solver of problems; you're the one who stays in control by keeping your head, asking the right questions, and being precise when it comes to giving necessary advice.

Lighten up and win! And remember: success couldn't happen to a nicer person.

Quick Reference Summary

Technique 1: Communicating the Message that It is Sound Business to Trust You

Don't cut corners at the expense of your own credibility – it's one of your most powerful weapons. You're not in the business of attracting gullible characters; you are in the business of building mutually beneficial long-term partnerships.

Technique 2: Asking the Right Questions

Ease in with simple questions that get the prospect talking about him or herself, then move on to the past, the present, and the future – complementing each with 'why?' and 'how?'. Use 'middle-ground' questions where appropriate, but beware of over-reliance on them. You must take the responsibility of keeping the cycle moving forward.

Technique 3: Taking the Lead

Tell the prospect where you are at any given point in the sales cycle. Don't be afraid to steer the conversation in the direction you want it to go. If there are questions or problems, you'll hear about them and that's what you want! When in doubt, take the initiative in a calm, professional manner.

Technique 4: Engaging the Prospect

Don't play ping-pong – work from the unique set of verbal and non-verbal cues your prospect will supply. Discuss subjects with which you are comfortable and familiar. Discuss the surroundings. 'Lean in' when the prospect begins to talk about himself. Show care by really caring.

Technique 5: Finding Key Requirements

'Find a need and fill it' has its limits. For most of us, the day of relying exclusively or primarily on first-time customers has passed. Find requirements you can fill among those sought-after, qualified buyers who know full well that the choice is theirs.

Technique 6: Converting the Leads that 'Fall into Your Lap'

The sale you deserve? Maybe. But take the time to establish a relationship and find out what's going on. Then ask to set up an appointment. Don't assume you're on to a 'sure thing!'

Technique 7: Knowing How to Make Your Product or Service Fit Somewhere Else

Does what you sell work in only one way? Or can you adjust it, make it serve some new purpose or function? Can you present it in a different light, or to a different group of people?

Technique 8: Pretending You're a Consultant (Because You Are)

Don't improvise. If you need to take time to come up with a workable solution, do so. Solving problems is the name of the game – and you have to listen before you can provide a solution.

Technique 9: Asking for the Next Appointment While You're on the First Visit

Perhaps the simplest, easiest-to-follow piece of advice in this book. Don't make excuses – make appointments!

Technique 10: Taking Notes

Taking notes during your meeting with the prospect helps you to listen, puts you in a position of authority, encourages your prospect to open up, and sends positive signals.

Technique 11: Creating a Plan With Each New Prospect

It may be routine for you, but the prospect has never gone through the sales cycle with you before. Produce a customised, written plan based on your notes from earlier meetings. Remember, you're the doctor – don't rush the diagnosis!

Technique 12: Asking for Referrals

Don't be shy – you can't afford it. Referrals are the lifeblood of a successful career in sales. Carry a packet of index cards with you at all times; say, 'I expect there are a number of people in your (industry, area, related businesses) who could benefit from my talking to them about this (product/service). Do you know of five people I could talk to?'

Technique 13: Showing Enthusiasm

Talk up your company – and remember that there is a difference between enthusiasm and poorly disguised panic. Enthusiasm builds bridges; panic tears them down.

Technique 14: Giving Yourself Appropriate Credit

Talk about yourself – but be humble. (No, the two aren't mutually exclusive.) Convey success, confidence, and flexibility. Highlight past successes, but don't try to outdo the prospect. Try to exhibit the characteristics of a person who makes things happen.

Technique 15: Telling the Truth (It's Easier to Remember)

We tell, on average, 200 white lies every day! Well, social conventions and pleasantries are one thing – misleading the prospect about your ability to meet a deadline is quite another. Remember, your credibility is a precious asset; defend it!

Technique 16: Selling Yourself on Yourself

Motivate yourself! Avoid the radio during your morning journey to work; listen to motivational tapes instead. Be specific with your goals – and your rewards. Get positive reinforcement. Leave yourself notes. Keep things in perspective.

Technique 17: Starting Early

There is a world before 9 am! You can beat the secretary trap, ease your journey to work, reduce your aggravation, and improve your attitude by getting in an hour or so before everyone else does. It may sound tough – try it anyway. You'll be a convert before you know it.

Technique 18: Reading Industry Publications (Yours and Your Clients')

Trade journals and newsletters are invaluable data sources; read them. These publications are fertile sources of leads, industry gossip, and all manner of important inside stuff – take advantage of them!

Technique 19: Supporting Your Visit the Next Day

Phone or write to your prospect the day after your visit. The vast majority of people who mean to do this never actually get around to it; build this step into your schedule!

Technique 20: Giving Speeches to Business and Civic Groups

You will benefit tremendously from the boost in confidence you receive from being treated as an expert in your field (which you are); in addition, an average of one in ten audience members will ask about your services.

Technique 21: Passing the Word When the Opportunity is Appropriate

Being a part of the 'grapevine' is a wise decision – one I've never heard any salesperson regret making.

Technique 22: Taking Responsibility For Presentations that Go Haywire

Rejected? Try this: 'Mr Jones, I just don't understand . . . I must have made a mistake in my presentation for you to make this decision. I know we can help you. Can you help *me* and show me where things went wrong?' You may have to put aside the common fixation with being 'right' – but, then again would you rather be 'right', or close a sale?

Technique 23: Being Honest with Yourself about the Nature of the Firm You Work For

If you have to choose between fighting a losing battle for losing generals and finding another army, find another army. Don't rationalise.

Technique 24: Telling Everyone You Meet Who You Work For and What You Sell.

Why not make a point of broadcasting your profession to anyone and everyone – with pride? This is not the same as subjecting everyone you meet to a sales pitch! Simply pass on your name, profession and company affiliation to every new person you meet.

Technique 25: Keeping Your Sense of Humour

It can be tough to be a salesperson sometimes – but that's exactly why sales work has to be funny now and then! Lighten up – and remember, success couldn't happen to a nicer person.

Further Reading from Kogan Page

The Best Seller, D Forbes Ley
Inspired Selling, J T Auer
Motivate to Win, Richard Denny
Secrets of Telephone Selling, Neil Johnson
Selling to Win: Tested Techniques for Closing the Sale, Richard
   Denny
Sell Your Way to the Top, Peter Thomson
Speak for Yourself, Richard Denny
The 25 Most Common Sales Mistakes . . . and How to Avoid Them,
   Stephan Schiffman